The Bells of Saint Babel's

POEMS 1997–2001

T0124415

The Bells of Saint Babel's

POEMS 1997–2001

ALLEN CURNOW

CARCANET

First published in 2001 by
Auckland University Press, New Zealand

Published in Great Britain in 2001 by
Carcanet Press Limited
4th Floor, Conavon Court
12–16 Blackfriars Street
Manchester M3 5BQ

A CIP catalogue record for this book
is available from the British Library

ISBN 1 85754 538 9

The publisher acknowledges financial assistance
from the Arts Council of England.

Printed and bound in England by SRP Ltd, Exeter

to Jeny

CONTENTS

Acknowledgements

Grateful acknowledgment is due to *London Review of Books*, which first published the following six of these poems: 'Ten Steps to the Sea', 'The Kindest Thing', 'The Cake Uncut', 'The Bells of Saint Babel's', 'A Nice Place on the Riviera' and 'Fantasia and Fugue for Pan-pipe'. An earlier version of 'The Cake Uncut' appeared in *2000 AD/ The Anthology*, published by the New Zealand *Sunday Star-Times*.

Three of the Four Poems after Pushkin were first published in *After Pushkin: Versions of the poems of Alexander Sergeevich Pushkin* by contemporary poets (ed. and introduced by Elaine Feinstein). I am grateful to The Folio Society and to Carcanet Press, publishers of the editions of that volume, for permission to reprint here 'When and Where', 'The Upas Tree', and 'The Talisman'. 'When and Where' also appeared in the *Times Literary Supplement*.

Thanks are likewise due to Bridgewater Press, as publishers, and Anthony Thwaite, as editor, of *Paeans for Peter Porter: a celebration for Peter Porter on his seventieth birthday by twenty of his friends*, for allowing me this use of 'A Pantoum for Peter at Seventy'.

My reading of 'The Pocket Compass' was recorded for the BBC at the spot described in the poem, my cottage on Lone Kauri Road, Karekare, Auckland. It was broadcast by BBC Radio 4 on 5 October 2000, in the course of a sequence of new sonnets commissioned for the National Poetry Day.

My Note on 'Fantasia and Fugue for Pan-pipe' owes a great deal to the textual advice of Dr W. R. Barnes, of the University of Auckland, concerning key passages in Plutarch and Eusebius, with commentary from various editions.

A.C.

Ten Steps to the Sea

I

Repeat this experience
wilfully.
Instruct this
experience to repeat
itself.

II

With or without
vicarious detail for all
verities of this place.
Me too.

III

Plenty of that
already. Kikuyu grass
underfoot, thunderheads, purple-
patched sunshine offshore, onshore
the high dunes, the hollows of
wetted sand, rabbit shit.
Foot of a cliff, arm of a stream
where fallen yellow bloom
degrades.
September sickness.
El Niño weather.

IV

One wild, white
arum leans landward a little, round
which in its pool, drip-fed off
a slimed rock-face, is arranged the sky
for inspection.

V

A remark
for the rising sun. I see
by what blinds me.

VI

Telling us about
his cancer, he said: 'They can control
the pain till there's well really
no pain, but then there's no reality.'
He said: 'I try to balance
the two, as little pain
as possible, as much reality
as possible.'

VII

One moment before
that cloud bursts and the flash
flood swipes, I'm across
safely, seeing stringers, planks,
gadarening down into the tide
which rises to receive them. There

goes our bridge. How the upstream
railing splintered, the deck duck-
diving, you'd never know now.
Good as new.

VIII

The pain is the dog
not heeding the whistle, on account
of scenting a rabbit or an old
turd, his own possibly, or snuffing
ashes of a Sunday campfire because of
the slab and the grate provided there.
Will he follow?

IX

Up and over the sandhills? Not much
help in the sea's habitual heave,
sprawl, grumble, hiss.

X

In reality,
no. A step in the right direction.
The pain is this wind, which blows the whole
time, uncontrollably.
In your face.

The Kindest Thing

Rear-vision glass
   knows what comes up

out of whatever
   concealed exit

I've left behind
   me. These cross-country

highways hide little
   for long, and least

when driving east
   one of those bright

spring mornings. Green
   acclivities drop

back. Sheep with them.
   What comes up next

comes fast, the ute
   probes left, probes right

(how can hurrying
   mirrors keep up?),

overtakes me
   with a long blast

storms past into full
   view carrying

at gathering speed
   what was concealed,

only heard, the dog
   half-hanged, roped

by the neck, raving,
   clawing at the tailboard

forefeet can't climb
   back over, hind-

legs cruelly danced
   off the tar-seal.

Bare road between us
   lengthens. Away

out of sight, how long
   will it have held,

that rope, till it parts?
   And the ute's gone,

the dog's flung down
    and I brake, short

of the strangely small
    body, the one

coin-size blood spot
    at the jaws. Convulsed,

gets to its feet.
    Convulsed, falls over.

And I'm joined here
    at the roadside by

the Maori boy who
    saw it all, from

that house, the first
    before Kawakawa.

Where there's a vet.
    Pick the dog up.

Put the dog down.
    These hurts can't heal.

At the vet's, yes,
    green with a white

logo on the cab.
    And he, not council

car? Got the number?
    And I, that speed!

You're joking *Drunk –*
stoned, more likely,

on the hemp, cash
    crop around here.

And he, Ranger's job,
    picking up strays.

We put them down.
    Kindest thing, most times.

The Cake Uncut

I

Not him – he's where
no fears can find

nor torments touch
him – it's his Mum

has the details,
who told the head-

master, who talked
to the press.

        Dad
only just gone

for the takeaways
at KFC,

when he says – quiet,
sort of sudden,

you'd hardly know
it was him speaking –

'Can't wait any more
for Dad, I've got

to go now – no,
just tired again,

like yesterday' – that
was when I knew

how it had to be,
like he said, *now*.

II

We're very religious
people. We sing,

we pray to God
to make the lump

go away, if that's
His will – it still

swells up, and up
so big you'd never

believe, it could
be a football

there in the leg.
The lady kept

at us, why don't
you see the doctor?

Try everything.
What harm can that

possibly do?
Made him sick – no

way would he keep
anything down –

medicine killing him, we
threw it all out.

Never went back.
No one's come near

till the police –
God knows we've done

nothing like what
they said – his life's

necessities – our own
heart's blood was his

if it would save him –
I always hear

him say *now*, the moment
before it was.

III

Funny dream.
                    Dad's
in bed with me
and that come-dom

thing on, and says
how do you like

my Mexican hat?
That's where we're going

when the Lotto money
comes, people get

cured there, like that
kid on the talkback –

something about
apricot stones –

IV

Shame not to cut the
cake with his twelve

candles on. God'll
have you up and running

again, for your
birthday, I'm saying

and we'll all see
the Millennium in –

he'd've loved that so,
every minute, even

knowing, all along,
what never was meant.

The Bells of Saint Babel's

After those months
at sea, we stank

worse than the Ark.
Faeces of all

species, God's first
creation, cooped

human and brute,
between wind and

water, bound for
this pegged-out plain

in the land called
Shinar, or some-

thing. Give or take
some chiliads, I'll

have been born there.
Saint Babel's tower

with spire (sundry
versions of that)

stuck not far short
of a top (Wait

for it!) gilded
to catch first light

or last flame flung
by the torched snows

farthest west.
                    Four
shiploads of us.

Under its breath
a warm land breeze,

wind of our coming,
breathed Shit!

Lightered ashore,
our cabin trunks,

rust-freckled steel-
braced outside, inside

compartments kept
things lavendered,

smothered memories
of sweats and smears.

For laters. Boxroom
dry dreams, our child-

hood's indoors, wet
holiday games . . .

2

We wanted it
above all (except

heaven) to make
the world out there

aware, if there's
any such world,

as if to cry
Look! Look at me!

Very old story.
Some other time.

Before all this.
Before history ran

out of excuses . . .

3

I, the present
writer, that is,

can see the Rev.
F.G. Brittan,

octogenarian
of stertorous

pulpit delivery,
who also told

the time by the ding
and the tink-tink

simply by a squeeze
of his silver watch:

seated beside
the vicarage fire

'after Service':
who, babe-in-arms

(his mother's) came
ashore that day

where four ships lay
under the steep

hills, beyond which
an unbuilt city was

unpaved wetlands,
too near, too far

from unclimbed alps.
Settlers made shift

improvising
themselves. In shock.

Still do. Still are.
Only the games

they play . . .

4
To relocate the
roof of the world,

obviously Everest
has to be moved –

South Latitude
thirty-three West

Longitude one-
seventy-seven, where

Kermadec Trench
ten thousand metres

deep floored with 'fine
volcanic ash,

aeolian dust'
drowns mountains.

New Zealand side
of the Date Line

meaning, those shores,
Raoul Island, any

Kermadec reef
cries to the sun,

Me! Me! This day
dawns first on me,

you won't find that
in your King James

nor Maori story
of a half-god's

trap for the sun,
that sun . . .
            which one?
Which thousand years?

5

Next time you look,
he will have stepped

out of the shade
the West Front casts

into a sun-stuffed
ambulatory called

Cathedral Square.
His buttoned black

gaiters encase
his shanks. The Dean

of Saint Babel's
rig of the day.

One more step, he's
joined by a friend,

silk hat, frock coat,
silver-knobbed cane.

Their morning walk.
What makes the tower

burst but thunderclappers
newly hung, high

peal deafeningly
detonating,

the Dean's delight,
Are not those bells

Divine?
        Silk hat,
hand cupped on ear,

shouts back, What's that?
and Gaiters, Divine!

And he, What? What?
Can't make it out –

Sorry, Mister Dean,
can't hear a word

for those DAMNED BELLS.

The Pocket Compass

(i.m. G.E.T.)

We stood at the timbered railing just one steep
rain-forested mile above the sea
the upper rail being level enough
to lay your pocket compass to copy there

the compass-rose, for me to get my bearings
by, for you to see our world the right
way round. The blaze of a late sun half
blinds us. Later, my chisel will have incised

the upper case cardinal points, years after that
the rotted rail will have been replaced,
pencil or chisel can't replicate
the rose in the mind's eye, indelibly true

north by needle. I paint it over again
in sight of the sea with one more sun to drown.

For Peter Porter at Seventy

a pantoum

Clock-watchers all for whom the digits tick
our momentsworth of years. Nine sevens brought
a six and a three and a Grand Climacteric.
Take one more seven, this one's next to a nought,

our momentsworth of years. Nine sevens brought
small pickings, and what's so special about ten?
Take one more seven, this one's next to a nought,
shall we count on time to fetch the same again?

Small pickings! And what's so special about ten
is the ninetieth psalm, that scary three-score *and*
shall we count on time to fetch the same again
like a birthday of the world, from where we stand?

Is the ninetieth psalm, that scary three-score *and*
ten years any good reason to rejoice
like a birthday of the world from where we stand?
new stars, in perfect time and excellent voice.

Ten years! Any good reason to rejoice,
day barely broken after that small Bang,
new stars in perfect time and excellent voice
sang together, together was how they sang.

Day barely broken after that small Bang
the young stars of your native Brisbane sky
sang together, together was how they sang
as we met, you fifty-plus, turned seventy I.

The young stars of your native Brisbane sky
out of our terrene earshot sang back shrilly
as we met, you fifty-plus, turned seventy I –
Consider the idle ant, the busy lily

out of our terrene earshot sang back shrilly,
ciphering note of an organ-pipe high wind –
consider, the idle ant, the busy lily
do nothing but rhyme – the high outback sound,

ciphering note of an organ-pipe high wind
continuo under the voice – your own, so many
do nothing but rhyme – the high outback sound
upfront, more of our hemispheres than any,

continuo under the voice – your own, so many
have made so few and fewer that come to mind
upfront more of our hemispheres than any –
And I, eight decades crowding me behind,

have made so few and fewer that come to mind –
a six and a three and a Grand Climacteric –
and I, eight decades crowding me behind,
clock-watchers all, for whom the digits tick.

Four Poems after Pushkin

I

WHEN AND WHERE

Where the big crowds come, the street,
the stadium, the park where the young
go crazy to the beat
and the heated bubble of the song,

thoughts running loose, I tell
myself, the years will have blipped past,
one by one the lot of us here present will
be gone into the dark. Someone's last

hour's always next, right here and now.
Deep under the bark of that great oak
my father's lifetime's told in rings, which grow
to outlive me too. Gently as I stroke

this child's head, I'm thinking, 'Goodbye!
It's all yours now, the season's crop —
your time to bud, and bloom, while my
late leaves wither and drop —'

And which day of which year
to come will turn out to have been
the anniversary, distant or near,
of my death? Good question. The scene,

will it be wartime, on a trip,
or at home or in some nearby
street, crashed coach or a ship-
wreck that I'm to die?

Cadavers couldn't care less where they rot,
yet the living tissue leans (as best it may)
toward the long-loved familiar spot
for its rest. Mine does, think of it that way.

Freshly dug. Young things, chase your ball.
Nature's not watching, only minding
by its own light perpetual
beauty of its own fact or finding.

1829

II

THE UPAS TREE

Scorched unforgiving soil
burned off burned out
in summer conflagrations

half-way to the horizon
look for the Upas Tree
no other created thing
to be seen than this

grim guard

           the parched
steppes convulsed
at its birth
and a deathly day that was
loading root and branch with
instant poison
visibly in the heat of noon
sweated out by nightfall
globuled and beaded
thick thick
           and clear
the concentrate
lethal
        the small birds
drop dead from the sky
outside the dripline of its leaves

the tiger
gives it a wide berth

only the black whirlwind
swarms up it and out again
with death to deliver
and any passing cloud
sprinkling its foliage
carries across the hot sand
its poisonous rain

'Find that tree
bring back the deadly stuff'
his imperial master said
and off he went
and by morning brought
one resinous lump
and one withering branch
and fell to the rush-strewn floor
of the great tent
to die at the feet
of his Lord now possessed of
invincible power

and that power made
him such murderous missiles
as devastated
neighbouring realms
and subjected
them and their peoples
by life's death-dealing arts.

1828

III

WINTER EVENING

This pig of a gale
     now screams, now drops
     to a baby's wail
     while it wraps
     cloud-cover around the sky
     where twisters of snow
     fall and flake as they fly.

Gusts fit to blow
     straws out of our thatch,
     or like someone's there
     at the window-catch
     stormbound, after dark –

dark enough in here,
     our tumbledown shack.

Grandmother dear,
     why wouldn't you speak
     just then as you sat
     by the window spinning?
     Was it nothing but that
     crazy wind's dinning?
     Had you just dropped off
     to the humming of the wheel?

Let's drink! That's the stuff
        to make us both feel
        better, old mate of my sad
        young life.
                Where's the jug?
Things can't be that bad.
Sing me the old songs,
the one about the blue
bird resting its wings
far across the sea,
the one about the girl
who got up so very early
before daybreak
to fetch water from the creek –

while this pig of a gale
now screams, now drops
to a baby's wail
and it wraps
cloud-cover around the sky
with its gusts that blow
those twisters of snow
that fall and flake as they fly.

Let's drink! little old
        friend of my unhappy
        youth, our glasses filled
        with the gladdening stuff
        smiling at grief.

1825

39

IV

THE TALISMAN

A warmer latitude.
An unvisited
beach.
    Rocks wetted where
the last wave broke.
        Some
such night as this lit
by a swollen moon's
foggy glow.
      Somewhere
the Pasha (of these parts)
relaxing sucks at the
narghile the sweet
fume inhaling.
       Was it
there this ravishingly
wise woman whose hands caressed
me pressed something small
into mine?
     Keep it.
It's a talisman.
Keep it safe. It's got
powers that love gave.
       Listen
while I tell you all
you need to know about

this precious thing.
                        Sick
it won't cure you. No
earthly use either in
the hour of death or day
of disaster.
                    Nor will it
win you the Lottery
crown you superstar
jet you happily home
(soured expatriate!) No.

But when cheating eyes
meet and you're aroused
oh my darling! (she said)
and lips after dark
unlovingly kiss
                    That's
when it kicks in – this
talisman of mine
                        you'll
never be two-timed
left for dead bleeding
newly from the heart!

1827

A Nice Place on the Riviera

The last act is bloody, however fine the rest of the play.
They throw earth over your head and it is finished for
ever. – Pascal, *Pensées*, XII.210 (tr. A. J. Krailsheimer).

I

Refuge in San
Remo won't work

out. Local health
officialdom rules

*La signora è
malata*. Not

welcome this side
of the frontier.

France is not far:
why don't I try

cousin Connie
Beauchamp? Nice place

they say they've got
in Menton. She

and inseparable
Jinnie Fullerton.

This horrible cough!
Kind souls. Perhaps

their prayers will work
with a few more Hail

Marys thrown in.
Connie or Jinnie

(never mind which)
murmured 'The Lord

has delivered you
into our hands'.

2

'No personal God
or any such

nonsense' – Katherine
Mansfield Beauchamp

to Murry, spouse,
from Villa Isola

Bella, Menton,
18 October

being much the age
Blaise Pascal was

(three centuries
back) to whom God

personally did
appear that day

'from about ten
thirty p.m.

till past midnight'.
Sick too. And wrote

'Fire', 'Jesus', 'God'
(ten times over) *and*

much more. They found
the parchment stitched

into his clothes
when they stripped him for

burial. Not known
like her, at this

address.

3

And there's
his *Pensées*, where

I left the book,
this rickety desk,

the Villa's one
spare room, kept up

in her name. Here
the annual New

Zealander sweats
brief tenure out,

memorialising
her genius. I

brought profound Blaise
along, whose death-

mask eyeballs me
glazedly, from

the paperback's
cover, with eyes

they plucked I (learn)
out of his painted

portrait and poked
them in here

and they look it.

4
Spring equinox:
lemon trees drenched

one minute, next
blast of the same

black sirocco
blow-dries bright green

under the shuttered
villa windows. Miss

Fullerton rose
from the escritoire,

having inscribed
her gift, the book,

from Jinnie, to
Katie, Saint

Joseph's day, nine-
teen twenty, *The*

*Imitation of
Christ*, (Thomas à

Kempis) in soft
red morocco,

title in gilt . . .
One Turkey rug's

length separates
the two. The *bonne*

brings coffee, liqueur.
That rabid wind

bangs shutters, dis-
colours the sea,

dishevels the world
outdoors. Beside

the demitasses
the Abdullahs in

their silver box,
the *Imitation*

waits to be read . . .
The climate here's

her only hope,
some doctor said.

Always a chance.

5

Your call, says Blaise.
Heads, there's God;

Tails, none. The coin
infinitely far

away spins itself
asleep, a still

spherical blur –
slowing, splits down

meridians, falls
over, face down,

face up. Your call.
God knows the odds

incalculably. Tell
me what your plans

are, for retirement.

6

Pieces of his mind
by the thousand,

jottings on jumbo-
size sheets. Pierced

for threading string.
Tied in *liasses*.

Too sick, or just
ran out of time

sorting the huge
heap. Such heads as

PROOFS OF JESUS,
NATURE CORRUPT,

SO ARE WE ALL,
CAUSES, EFFECTS . . .

7

Imitation – big
ask – of the life

he lived, the death
he died – if that

doesn't make two
of us, there's one

Christ lookalike
more than we knew.

8

Top-heavy *Alpes
Maritimes* grind

the sky small. Fast
forward, to autumn.

One of those two
women, who could

be seen watchfully
to cross the rail

tracks where they start
threading the rock

through to Liguria
halts, chestily coughs

in her handkerchief:
but has finished

writing her last
storybook; by now

consumption's two
years' gallop away

from Gurdjieff's
Institute, that

fatal torrential
haemorrhage, at

Fontainebleau,
stumbling upstairs.

9

Fast forward again
top-heavy *Alpes*

Maritimes grind
the sky small. One

more dull day scraped
off a slaty sea.

Fantasia and Fugue for Pan-pipe

I

Engaged too long
too chastely. Was

that it? Anyway,
she broke it off,

my father wrote
'Pan', earliest verse

of his, to make
it into print

over his name,
the god revealed

as Tremayne M.,
Syrinx as Maud.

Twenty-odd pages
further on, more

forgotten poems
between his lines

and hers (called 'Song'),
both plaintively

lovelorn, obscurely
set down between

Oceanian winds
and waters. *New*

Zealand Verse. Walter
Scott Publishing.

London. New York.
1906 – Safe

distances, for
blushing unseen,

big breaths unheard,
'O cruel nymph' not

unwritten and
much more, his drift

of 'low-blown music' –
the words, the lips,

the pipes – 'who love
thee still' – so eaves-

dropping Nature
guessed, or his poem

supposes – Maud's
chips in, crying over

spilt 'joyous youth
gone in a night'.

Her feral horned
god's hinderparts

wore clerical grey
serge, irreversibly

decent disguise.
Afterwards (not

long) that *traveller
came by . . . he took*

her with a sigh . . . his?
hers? or theirs?

II

Had a hand groped,
grabbed, come away

with a moist fist-
ful to play black

hole tunes, the ones
Pan pistol-whips

the galaxies with?
Terrified mind

whines to itself
don't panic, don't –

answers the hoof-
beat. Words for things,

things back again off
the tips of tongues.

Lost names. Try not to
think about that.

III

One world war later.
Not any more

the slender reed,
fifty-something Syrinx

drops in on one
newly-wed son

of Pan. I see
her, to my (not

small) surprise, seat
herself heavily

down on the foot
of the bed, hands

compress the ball
of a hanky, damp

from dabbing tear-
ducts. Someone said

she tells fortunes in
teashops, the dregs

of emptied cups,
to make ends meet. –

More tea? – quick look
at her watch – Oh,

thank you, no,

I'm running late, I
really must go.

IV

One lizard's wink,
two thousand years

(rounded out), since
Jesus called out

with a loud voice
it was all over,

that louder voice
downloads, this Greek

seaway hears GREAT
PAN IS DEAD – what

could be figured?
Who's being fingered?

And why's it got
so suddenly dark?

Nothing but those
four words themselves,

nobody spoke.
Printed now, like

Tremayne's, Maud's, mine.
Rolled up the beach

in a bottle, rolled
back into the surf.

Hoofprints in soft
and softening sand.

NOTES

Barring some likelier guess (or proof?) I am left with my own, which is that the story of the 'celebrated poison-tree of Macasser' could have reached Pushkin by way of Erasmus Darwin, the English botanist poet (grandfather of the more famous Charles) who had it from the report of a ship's surgeon, the Dutchman N. P. Foersch, published by the *London Magazine* of December 1783. Darwin's long poem, 'The Loves of the Plants' (1789, 4th edn. 1794) tells how '. . . on the blasted heath/ Fell Upas sits, the hydra-tree of death'. He bought the whole extraordinary tale of the tree's biocidal powers, and wrote: 'This however is certain, though it may appear incredible, that from 15 to 18 miles round this tree, not only no human creature can exist, but that, in that space of ground, no living animal of any kind has ever been discovered . . . there are no fish in the waters, nor has any rat, mouse, or other vermin, been seen there; and when birds fly near this tree, they fall a sacrifice to the effects of the poison'. Pushkin transplants his Upas from Java to a steppes region of vast extent: its birth and growth are imaged as startlingly as its deadly effects; but it is man, in the person of a pitiless despot, a Tsar, who finds his own use for it, its potential (so to speak) in biochemical weaponry. The poem is dated 1828. While adding a story of his own, with its own satirical spin, to the tales about the Upas, he need not have troubled much about degrees of credibility. A modern dictionary entry, by the way, correctly mentions its 'poisonous milky sap', also indicated by its scientific name, *Antiaris toxicaria*, and its known use for poisoned arrows.

For biblical allusions in (1) see Genesis chs. 10, 11. My '. . .
pegged-out plain/ in the land called/ Shinar . . . ' may be identified,
by a reader who happens to know the place and the history, with
the newly named Canterbury Plains in the South Island of New
Zealand, and the 'four ships' with the first arrivals of the Canter-
bury Association settlers in 1850: who also set about building a
Tower (with a 200ft spire) 'to make us a name, lest we be scattered'.
Like the colonists of Shinar, the builders of Babel, they were
generations shaped by a long voyage in unknown waters: one of
them was F. G. Brittan, named in (3). The vicarage where he sits at
the fireside still stands but is no longer a vicarage, and the timbered
parish church that stood nearby now serves as an assembly hall to a
city school some miles away. (4) The 'half-god' is Maui, most
famous hero in Polynesian mythology, where a well-known story
tells how he lengthened the day for the good of mankind, by
casting a noose round the neck of the sun-god, slowing down his
passage across the heavens. Maui stole fire, like Prometheus, and
like Proteus could change his shape into that of any other living
creature; he fished up the North Island of New Zealand (aka *Te Ika
a Maui*, Maui's fish). His hubristic challenge to the Goddess of
Death (*Hine nui te Po*, Great Woman of the Night) was the end of
him: his plan was to catch her asleep, and having taken the shape of
a caterpillar, to penetrate between her legs; but the cry of a bird
woke her and she crushed him there. In some versions the goddess
strangles Maui, or tears him in the terrible jaws of her *vagina
dentata*.

i-iii: ' . . . (Mercury) still had to tell what Pan said to the nymph, and how she, scorning his prayers, ran off through the pathless forest till she came to the still waters of sandy Ladon . . . prayed her sisters of the stream to transform her; and when Pan thought he had at last caught hold of Syrinx, he found that instead of the nymph's body he held a handful of marsh reeds. As he stood, sighing, the wind blew through the reeds, producing a thin, plaintive sound. The god was enchanted by this new device and the sweetness of the music . . . then he took reeds of unequal length and fastened them together with wax . . . ' (Ovid, *Metamorphoses* Book I, tr. Mary Innes).

i: . . . '*traveller/ came by . . . he took/ her with a sigh* . . . ' (William Blake, 'Never seek to tell thy love').

iv: '. . . since/Jesus called out/*with a loud voice/* it was all over, . . .' (cf. Gospels, Mark 16.34; John 19.30. King James version).

iv: '. . . this Greek/ seaway hears GREAT/ PAN IS DEAD. . . ' '(heard) from the island of Paxi the voice of someone loudly calling Thamus . . . an Egyptian pilot not known by name even to many on board . . . and the caller, raising his voice, said, "When you come opposite Palodes, announce that Great Pan is dead". . . . Thamus made up his mind, that if there should be a breeze, he would sail past and keep quiet, but with no wind and a smooth sea about the place he would announce what he had heard. . . . So, when he came opposite Palodes, and there was neither wind nor wave, Thamus from the stern, looking towards the land, said the words as he had heard them, "Great Pan is dead". . . . Even before he had finished there was a great cry of lamentation, not of one person but of many, mingled with exclamations of amazement. As many persons were on the vessel, the story was soon spread abroad in Rome, and Thamus was sent for by Tiberius Caesar (who) became so convinced of the truth of the story that he caused an investigation to be made about Pan; and the scholars, who were numerous at his court, conjectured that he was the son born of the god Mercury (Hermes) and Penelope . . . ' (Plutarch, AD c.50–125, *Moralia*, Loeb English translation). It was two centuries later that Eusebius, bishop of Caesarea, famous early Church historian, placed a Christian interpretation on the story: the death of 'Great Pan' signified the end of ancient paganism; the time of Tiberius coincided with the end of Christ's work on earth, with the downfall of the devils, as the old gods were seen to be by Christians. 'Great Pan' could be compared with the supreme Nature god known to the Stoics as Zeus-Cosmos, in some sense foreshadowing Christian doctrine. He was not (as Plutarch had supposed) one of the godlike *daimones*, still less the goat-like ('hairy') Pan worshipped by Arcadian shepherds. More than a thousand years after Eusebius, Rabelais again retells Plutarch's story, insisting that 'Great Pan' is none other than Jesus Christ: I quote from Peter Motteux's 17th century translation of *Pantagruel*, Book IV ch. 28, 'And methinks, my interpretation is not improper; for he may lawfully be said in the Greek tongue to be PAN, since he is our ALL. He is the god Pan, the great shepherd. The time also concurs . . . for this most good, this most mighty Pan, our only Saviour, died near Jerusalem during the reign of Tiberius Caesar'. Motteux could have picked up 'mighty Pan' from Spenser, who uses the identical phrase in *The Shepheardes Calender* (1579) or from Milton (who most probably did have it from Spenser) in 'On the Morning of Christ's Nativity' (1629):

> The shepherds on the lawn,
> Or ere the point of dawn,
> Sat simply chatting in a rustic row;
> Full little thought they than
> That the mighty Pan
> Was kindly come to live with them below . . .